Flip for Word Work
Phonics, Spelling, and Vocabulary

by Emily Cayuso

Maupin House *by*
capstone
professional

Flip for Word Work: Phonics, Spelling, and Vocabulary
by Emily Cayuso

Layout/Design by Mickey Cuthbertson
Illustrations by Josh Clark

Library of Congress Cataloging-in-Publication Data

Cayuso, Emily, 1954-
  Flip for word work : phonics, spelling, and vocabulary / by
Emily Cayuso.
      p. cm.
  Includes bibliographical references.
  ISBN-13: 978-0-929895-97-0 (table-top book design)
  ISBN-10: 0-929895-97-5
  1. Reading comprehension. I. Title.
LB1050.45.C3914 2007
372.47--dc22

                        2006027949

Also by Emily Cayuso:
  Flip for Comprehension
  Dar la Vuelta a la Comprensión
  Designing Teacher Study Groups

ISBN-10: 0-929895-97-5
ISBN-13: 978-0-929895-97-0

Printed in China by Color Craft Ltd., Hong Kong

Maupin House Publishing, Inc.
1710 Roe Crest Drive
North Mankato, MN 56003
888-262-6135
www.maupinhouse.com

Publishing Professional Resources that Improve Classroom Performance

Printed in China.
052014   008267

Table of Contents

Phonics Activities

Spelling Activities

Table of Contents (cont'd.)

Vocabulary Activities

Introduction

Words are the foundation of reading and learning, the tools we use to communicate ideas and learn new concepts. A student's word knowledge, then, is crucial to reading comprehension and future academic success. We can improve word recognition and spelling by finding ways to help students actively develop stronger vocabularies (Texas Education Agency, 2000).

This book is designed to provide teachers with ready-to-use word-work ideas that can be done as an extension to phonics, spelling, and vocabulary lessons. The hands-on activities enhance word-work exercises related to shared reading and can be used in various classroom settings.

Reading Groups: Use these activities with small reading groups as an extension of vocabulary, phonics, and spelling lessons related to the text the group is reading. The word-work activities can be used before, during, or after class reading.

Literacy Centers: Use this book as a stand-alone word-work center or add it to an existing writing, listening, or independent reading center. The activities in this resource enhance and expand literacy-center work.

Literature Circles: Ideas presented in the vocabulary section of this book can be used to facilitate class discussion and/or structure written responses and projects related to the vocabulary found in reading texts.

Introduction (cont'd.)

Shared Reading: Use these activities to facilitate, enhance, and extend student problem-solving strategies at the phonics level, as well as their understanding of new or unfamiliar vocabulary.

Phonics and Spelling: The phonics and spelling sections of the text can be used as whole-class activities during weekly phonics and spelling instruction or as homework assignments.

Model these activities with your students first, followed by sufficient teacher-guided practice before students are expected to complete them independently. Word-work exercises can be written out or performed orally. They can also be used as a guide for whole-group discussion, or you can ask students to complete the activities independently in their reading journals, on chart paper, or on construction paper. Likewise, the assignments can be completed in student pairs or small cooperative groups.

The exercises in *Flip for Word Work* are listed alphabetically and categorized as phonics, spelling, or vocabulary activities. Read the exercises and identify the particular word-work needs you want to address. Perhaps your teacher's guide suggests an idea similar to the ones you will find here. Certain reading texts naturally lend themselves to a particular activity, depending on the phonics patterns and vocabulary presented in the story. However you make your selections, remember that finding ways to improve word-work strategies for all readers is the goal.

How to Use This Book

- Use this book with a small group, whole class, or as part of an independent center.

- Stand the text up like a tent and turn to the exercise you want your students to practice.

- Insert any other information needed directly onto the page using sticky notes or cover-up tape. You may also clip a clear transparency sheet over the page and write on it.

- Model with your students how to successfully complete each activity.

- Provide the necessary materials to complete each activity.

Abbreviations

- **Use this week's reading text to locate abbreviations.**

- **Make a chart like the one below and write down the words you find.**

- **Add other abbreviations to your list.**

- **Use each abbreviation in a sentence.**

- **Read your list to your partner.**

Abbreviation	Word it Represents	Sentence
1. Mr.	Mister	Mr. Olsen lives next door.
2.		
3.		

Alliteration

- **Use the following letters your teacher has selected.**

- **Write an alliterative sentence with each letter provided. Remember, each word in your sentence should begin with the same letter sound.**

- **Draw a picture to illustrate your favorite sentence.**

- **Read your sentences to your partner.**

Elephants enjoy eating eggs.

Compound Words

- **Use this week's reading text to locate compound words.**

- **Make a chart like the one below and write down the words you find.**

- **Add other compound words to your list.**

- **Read your list to your partner.**

Word Part	Word Part	Compound Word
base	ball	baseball
after	noon	afternoon

Consonant Blends

- **Use this week's reading text to locate words containing the consonant blends listed below.**

- **List the blends on a chart like the one below.**

- **Add other words containing the same blends to the chart.**

- **Read your words to your partner.**

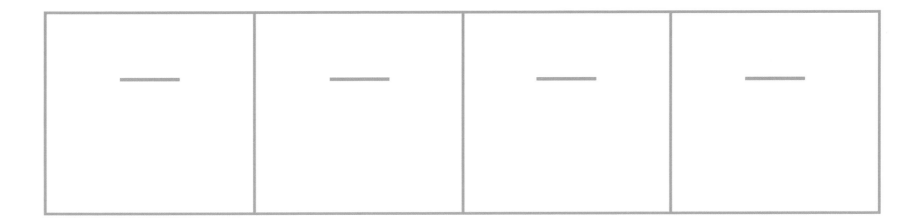

Contractions

- **Use this week's reading text to locate contractions.**

- **Write the contractions on a chart like the one below.**

- **Divide each contraction into its two separate words.**

- **Add other contractions to your list.**

- **Read your list to your partner.**

1st word	2nd word	Contraction
can	not	can't
was	not	wasn't

Digraphs

- **Use this week's reading text to locate words containing the consonant digraphs *ch*, *sh*, *th*, and *wh*.**

- **Make a chart like the one below and write down the words you find.**

- **Add other words containing digraphs to each list.**

- **Read your words to your partner.**

ch	sh	th	wh

Homophones

- **Use this week's reading text to locate homophones.**

- **Write the homophones on a chart similar to the one below.**

- **Write a sentence using each homophone.**

- **Add other homophones to your list.**

- **Read your list to your partner.**

Homophones	Sentences
here, hear	Bring the book **here**. I could not **hear** what you said.

Hunting for Vowels

- Use this week's reading text to locate words containing the vowel pattern your teacher has selected, such as *ou*, *ea*, *ee*, or *ai*.

- Write the words down.

- Add other words to your list that contain the same vowel pattern.

- Pick four words from your list and write a sentence for each on the back of your paper.

- Draw a picture to go with your sentences.

Making Words 1

● **Use the following letters your teacher has selected.**

● **Rearrange the letters to make as many words as you can. Write them on a sheet of paper.**

● **Look for similar patterns in the words you made, and, on the back of the sheet of paper, sort your words into categories.**

● **Label the categories.**

● **Add other words that fit into each category.**

Onomatopoeia

- Take a sheet of paper and fold it into eight boxes. You may make more if you like.

- Use this week's reading text to locate onomatopoeia words (words that imitate the sounds they represent).

- Write one word in each box and draw a picture to illustrate the sound each word makes.

- Add more onomatopoeia words to your paper.

Plurals

- **Use this week's reading text to locate plural words.**

- **Make a chart like the one below and write down the words you find.**

- **Add other plural words to your list.**

- **Use each plural word in a sentence.**

- **Read your list to your partner.**

Plural	Root word	Ending	Sentence
1. crabs	crab	s	We caught **crabs** at the beach.
2.			
3.			

Possessives

- **Use this week's reading text to locate possessives.**

- **Write the possessives on a chart similar to the one below.**

- **Identify the possessive as a singular or plural possessive.**

- **Write a sentence using each possessive.**

- **Add other possessives to your list.**

- **Read your list to your partner.**

Possessive	Singular or Plural	Sentence
dog's	singular	The **dog's** bone is gone.

Prefixes

- **Use this week's reading text to locate words with these prefixes:**

- **Make a chart like the one below and write down the words you find.**

- **Add other words containing similar prefixes to your list.**

- **Read your list to your partner.**

Prefix	Base Word	Word	Meaning
re	do	redo	to do again
un	happy	unhappy	not happy

Read and Write the Room

- Take a piece of paper and a clipboard and walk around the room looking for the letter, word pattern, or category your teacher has selected from the next page.

- Write your words on your clipboard.

- Pick four words from your list and write a sentence for each on the back of your paper.

- Draw a picture to go with each of your sentences.

Read and Write the Room (cont'd.)

- ❑ Short vowels
- ❑ Long vowels
- ❑ R-controlled vowels
- ❑ Double consonants
- ❑ Prefixes
- ❑ Suffixes
- ❑ Plurals
- ❑ Possessives
- ❑ Abbreviations
- ❑ Titles
- ❑ Pronouns
- ❑ Homophones
- ❑ Contractions
- ❑ Synonyms
- ❑ Antonyms
- ❑ Rhyming words

- ❑ Consonant digraphs
- ❑ Consonant blends
- ❑ Number words
- ❑ Color words
- ❑ Days and months
- ❑ Nouns
- ❑ Proper nouns
- ❑ Verbs
- ❑ Adjectives
- ❑ Adverbs
- ❑ Compound words
- ❑ One-syllable words
- ❑ Two-syllable words
- ❑ Three-syllable words
- ❑ Four-syllable words
- ❑ _____

Suffixes

● **Use this week's reading text to locate words with these suffixes:**

● **Make a chart like the one below and write down the words you find.**

● **Add other words containing similar suffixes to your list.**

● **Read your list to your partner.**

Base Word	Suffix	Word
jump	ing	jumping
play	ed	played
like	s	likes

Using Spelling Patterns

- Take a sheet of paper and fold it into boxes.

- Write one spelling pattern at the top of each box.

- See how many other words you can make that contain the same spelling pattern and write them in the box.

ea	ee	
bean	feet	
neat	meeting	
meal	see	
sea	cheek	

Spelling patterns to use:

Word Families 1

- Use the patterns your teacher has selected from the next page to make word families like the ones below.

- Write your word families on sentence strips or adding machine tape.

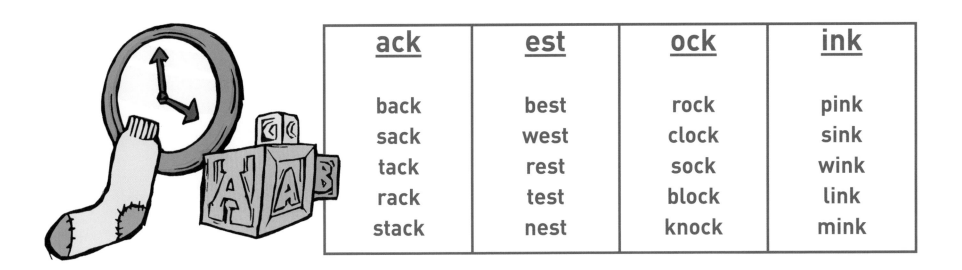

ack	est	ock	ink
back	best	rock	pink
sack	west	clock	sink
tack	rest	sock	wink
rack	test	block	link
stack	nest	knock	mink

Word Families 1 (cont'd.)

- ☐ ack
- ☐ ail
- ☐ ain
- ☐ ake
- ☐ ale
- ☐ all
- ☐ ame
- ☐ an
- ☐ ank
- ☐ ap
- ☐ ash
- ☐ _____

- ☐ at
- ☐ ate
- ☐ aw
- ☐ ay
- ☐ eat
- ☐ ell
- ☐ elt
- ☐ en
- ☐ end
- ☐ ess
- ☐ est
- ☐ _____

- ☐ ib
- ☐ ick
- ☐ ide
- ☐ ight
- ☐ ill
- ☐ in
- ☐ ine
- ☐ ing
- ☐ ink
- ☐ ip
- ☐ it
- ☐ _____

- ☐ ock
- ☐ oke
- ☐ op
- ☐ ore
- ☐ ot
- ☐ uck
- ☐ ug
- ☐ ump
- ☐ unk
- ☐ up
- ☐ ut
- ☐ _____

Writing Spree

- **Use a stop watch, sand timer, or clock with a second hand to time your writing spree.**

- **Take a sheet of paper and write as many words as you can that contain the spelling pattern your teacher selects. Give yourself two minutes and race against your partner.**

- **Use a dictionary to check your answers.**

Circle Time

- **Write your spelling words down and circle the part of the word that your teacher has selected from the list below.**

- **Write more words with the same part. Circle the part.**

☐ Base word   ☐ R-controlled vowels

☐ Prefix   ☐ Syllables

☐ Suffix   ☐ Double consonants

☐ Digraphs   ☐ Double vowels

☐ Consonant blends   ☐ Compound words

☐ Short vowels   ☐ Word within a word

☐ Long vowels   ☐ _____

Closed Spelling Sort

- **Sort your spelling words according to the method your teacher has selected below.**

- **Make a chart to illustrate your sort.**

- **Add other words that fit in each sort category.**

☐ Number of letters
☐ Initial consonant
☐ Short vowel sounds
☐ Long vowel sounds
☐ Number of syllables
☐ Suffixes
☐ Prefixes
☐ Digraphs

☐ Consonant blends
☐ R-controlled vowels
☐ Double consonants
☐ Double vowels
☐ Word meaning/ concept
☐ _____ and _____
☐ _____, _____, and _____
☐ ____, _____, ___, and _____

Cloze Sentences

- **Write a sentence for each spelling word, replacing the spelling word with a blank.**

- **Exchange sentences with your partner.**

- **Your partner will fill in the blanks with the correct spelling word.**

- **You may keep score by awarding points for each correct sentence.**

1. Use the _____ to pay for the book.
2. That car was in a bad _____ .
3. I love to eat _____ potatoes.

crash   cash   mashed

Guess a Word

- Choose a word from your spelling list and select magnetic letters that spell the word.

- Mix up the letters and pass them to your partner.

- Have your partner guess the word and spell it correctly using the letters.

- Write the spelling word on a sheet of paper.

- Take turns with all your spelling words. Keep score if you like.

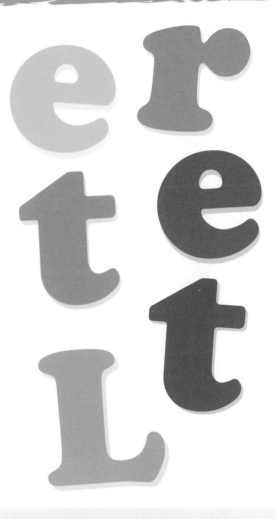

NOTE TO TEACHERS: This activity can also be done with high-frequency word lists.

Letter Writing

- **Write a letter to a classmate using as many spelling words as you can.**

- **Don't forget the parts of a letter.**

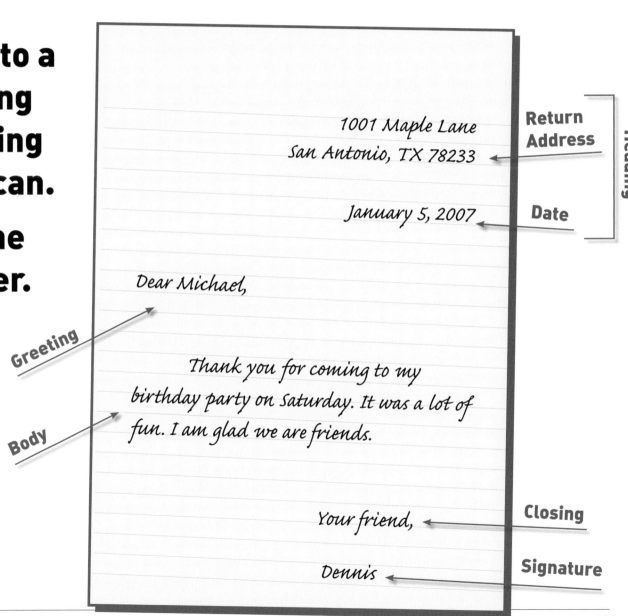

1001 Maple Lane
San Antonio, TX 78233 — **Return Address**

Heading

January 5, 2007 — **Date**

Dear Michael, — **Greeting**

Thank you for coming to my birthday party on Saturday. It was a lot of fun. I am glad we are friends. — **Body**

Your friend, — **Closing**

Dennis — **Signature**

Magazine and Newspaper Hunt

- **Find your spelling words in old magazines and newspapers.**

- **Highlight the words when you locate them.**

- **You earn two points for each word you find.**

- **Write the words down when finished and add up your points.**

NOTE TO TEACHERS: This activity can also be done with high-frequency word lists.

Words	Points

Making Words 2

- **Take a sheet of paper and fold it into boxes.**

- **Write one spelling word at the top of each box.**

- **See how many other words you can create using the letters in your spelling word.**

- **Write them in the box.**

radish	finish	
dish	fish	
dash	in	
hid	fin	
rid	shin	

Open Spelling Sort

- Sort your spelling words by whatever method you like.

- Make a chart to illustrate your sort. Label the categories.

- Add other words that fit in each category you created.

My Open Sort

Quotations

- **Write sentences that include quotations using each of your spelling words.**

- **Draw a picture to illustrate your favorite sentence.**

"I'm <u>lost</u>," said the little girl to the policeman.

Spelling Acrostics

- **Choose a spelling word from your list.**

- **Write an acrostic poem based on the word.**

- **Start each line with a different letter of the word. Be as creative as you can.**

- **Draw a picture to illustrate your poem.**

Bubbles are fun to make.

Use a wand to dip in soap.

Begin to blow slowly.

Blow a little more.

Let it get bigger.

Explosion!

Spelling Sentence Cut-ups

- **Write a sentence for each of your spelling words on a strip of paper (you may also use a sentence strip or adding-machine tape).**

- **Take each sentence and cut it apart word by word. Put the words in an envelope or small plastic bag.**

- **Exchange sentences with your partner and reassemble them correctly.**

- **You may keep score by awarding points for each correct sentence.**

Story Time

Using as many of your spelling words as you can, write a story in the genre your teacher has selected.

- ❑ Fiction
- ❑ Non-fiction
- ❑ Historical Fiction
- ❑ Fairy Tale
- ❑ Autobiography
- ❑ Scary Story
- ❑ Fable

- ❑ Tall Tale
- ❑ Animal Story
- ❑ Nursery Rhyme
- ❑ Mystery
- ❑ Play
- ❑ Science Fiction
- ❑ Comedy

Using a Thesaurus

- **Make a chart like the one below.**

- **Write your spelling words in the first column.**

- **Reference a thesaurus to find interesting synonyms for the spelling words and write them in the second column.**

- **On the back of your paper pick your favorite synonyms and use them in sentences. Draw a picture to go with each sentence you write.**

Spelling Words	Synonyms

Word Families 2

- **Take a sheet of paper and fold it into boxes.**

- **Write one spelling word at the top of each box.**

- **In each box, write other words that rhyme with the spelling word.**

<u>hill</u>	<u>wall</u>	<u>spell</u>
fill	ball	sell
will	tall	tell
still	call	well

Word Ladders

- **Take a sheet of paper and write one of your spelling words at the top (you may also use a sentence strip or adding-machine tape).**

- **Under the first word, write a new word by changing or rearranging the letters in the first word.**

- **To make the next word on the ladder, change or rearrange the letters of the last word written.**

My Word Ladder

Shop
Ship
Hips
Hops
Soap
Soak
Sack
Sick
Kick
Icky
Icy

Book Review

- **Write a summary of the text you are reading this week.**

- **In your summary description, include ALL the new vocabulary words that were introduced in the text.**

Write a description of the setting.	
Write a description of the main characters.	
Write a description of the problem.	
Write a description of the resolution.	

Change a Paragraph

- **Choose a paragraph from the text you are reading and copy it on a sheet of paper.**

- **Make the paragraph dazzle by changing some of the ordinary words and phrases to more interesting ones. You may use a dictionary or thesaurus to help you.**

- **Rewrite the paragraph.**

- **Share your paragraph with your partner.**

Before	After
The boy walked down the hall even though he knew he was late. When he reached the door, he put his hand on the knob and went right in. Everyone looked at him.	The lad strolled down the hall even though he was aware he was tardy. When he arrived at the door, he grabbed the knob and barged right in. Everyone turned and stared in amazement.

Idioms

- **Make a chart like the one below.**

- **Use this week's reading text to locate idioms.**

- **Write the idioms on the chart.**

- **Illustrate the literal meaning of the idiom on one side of the chart and the figurative meaning on the other.**

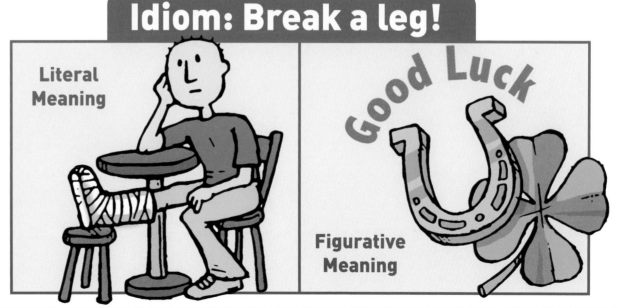

Idiom: Break a leg!

Literal Meaning

Good Luck

Figurative Meaning

Multiple Meaning Words

- **Make a star like the one shown.**

- **In the center of the star, write the vocabulary word your teacher gives you.**

- **Use a dictionary and find all the possible meanings of the word. Write the definitions on each point.**

- **Turn the star over, and write the vocabulary word in a sentence that illustrates each definition.**

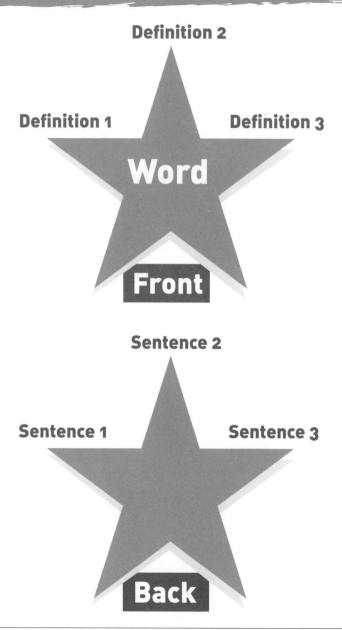

Definition 2

Definition 1   Definition 3

Word

Front

Sentence 2

Sentence 1   Sentence 3

Back

Picture Vocabulary

- Fold a sheet of paper into eight boxes. You may make more if you like.

- Find all the words that were new or hard for you to understand from your text and write them down, one word per box.

- Draw a picture that illustrates the word's meaning.

- Using your own words, write a definition of the word.

- Use your text or a dictionary to help you.

Root Word Webbing

- Make a web like the one shown.

- Write the root word that your teacher supplies in the center of the web.

- Root Word: _____

- Brainstorm related words that contain the root word.

- Add them to the web. You may use your text, a dictionary, or a thesaurus for help.

- On the back of your web, write a sentence using each word.

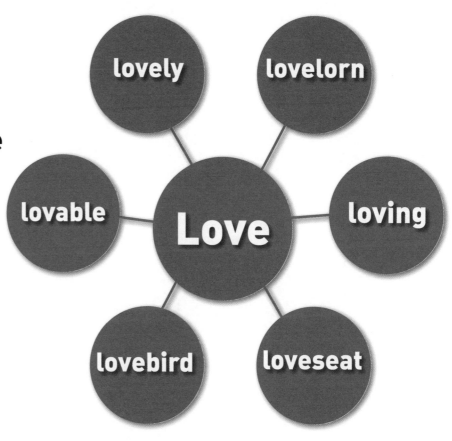

Semantic Web

- Make a web like the one shown.

- Write a new or unfamiliar word from the text you are reading in the center of the web.

- Brainstorm words and concepts that are in the same semantic (meaning) family as the word you wrote.

- Add them to the web. You may use your text, a dictionary, or a thesaurus for help.

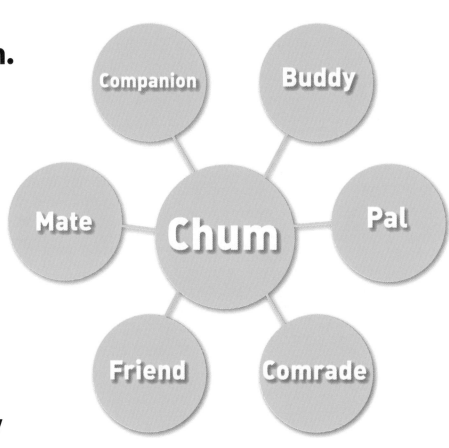

Similes and Metaphors

- **Make a chart like the one below.**

- **Use this week's reading text to locate similes and metaphors.**

- **Write the similes and/or metaphors on the chart.**

- **Fill in the rest of the chart.**

Simile/Metaphor	What is Compared	Meaning	Picture
1. A good book is like a good meal.	A book and a meal	A book can be as mentally satisfying as a good meal is physically satisfying.	
2.			

Visualizing Vocabulary

- Draw a picture or diagram of the _____ that was talked about in the text.

- Label its parts with the correct vocabulary word.

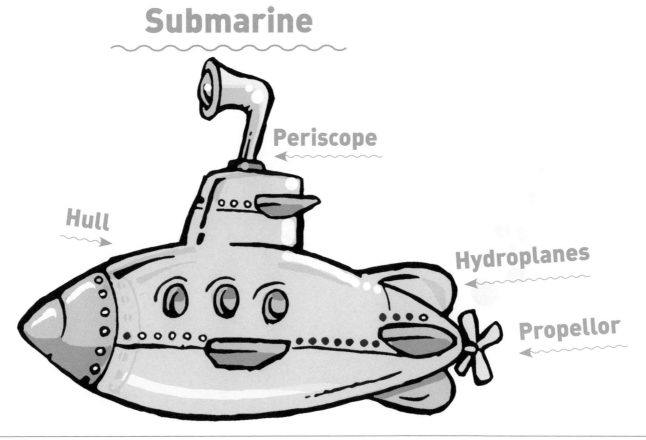

Submarine

Periscope

Hull

Hydroplanes

Propellor

Vocabulary Inferences

- **Make a chart like the one below.**

- **In the first section, write down words from your text that are tricky or hard to understand.**

- **In the middle section, write what you infer the word means.**

- **In the last section, write what helped you to make that inference.**

Word	What I Think It Means	What Helped Me
1.		
2.		
3.		
4.		

Vocabulary KWL

- **Fill out the first two sections of the KWL chart before reading your text.**

- **Fill out the last two sections when you finish reading.**

Vocabulary I Know about the Subject	Vocabulary I Want to Know	Vocabulary I Learned	Where I Learned It

Vocabulary Log

- Create a vocabulary log for the text you are currently reading.

- As you read the text, select words that are new or hard for you to understand and add them to your log.

- For each new word you add, include the information your teacher has checked below.

- Be ready to share your log when you have completed reading the text.

❏ the page the word is on
❏ the sentence the word is in
❏ the definition of the word

❏ a picture illustrating the word
❏ synonyms for the word
❏ what helped you determine the meaning of the word

Vocabulary Quick Draw

- **Put the vocabulary words to be learned in a hat.**

- **Take turns drawing a word from the hat.**

- **Draw the meaning of the word in pictures (NO WORDS).**

- **See if your partner can guess the word you drew.**

- **You may keep score if you like.**

Vocabulary Riddles

- Take one index card for each vocabulary word your teacher gives you.

- On the front of the card write a riddle for the word.

- On the back of the card write the word.

- Exchange your stack of cards with your partner, keeping the cards face up.

- Let your partner read each riddle and then try to guess the right vocabulary word without looking.

- You may keep score if you like.

You feel this way when your dog is lost but not when he is found.

Forlorn

Going away to camp can make you feel this way, no matter how much fun it is during your stay.

Homesick

Vocabulary Square

Pick a word that was new or hard for you to understand. Make a Vocabulary Square.

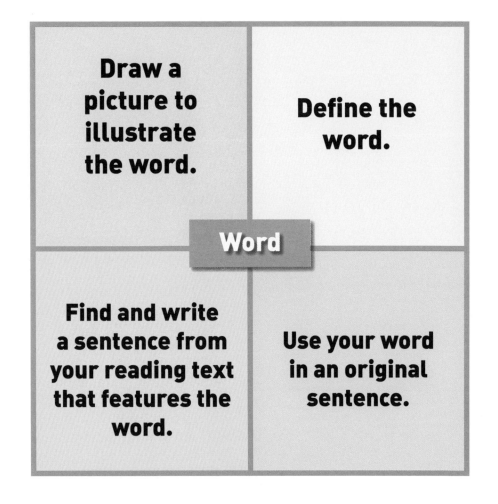

Draw a picture to illustrate the word.

Define the word.

Word

Find and write a sentence from your reading text that features the word.

Use your word in an original sentence.

Word Associations

Make connections with this week's vocabulary words by filling out a chart similar to this one.

Vocabulary Words	Meaning Connections	Visual Connections	Personal Connections
vehicle	It means the same as <u>car</u> or <u>auto</u>.	<u>Vehicle</u> ends like <u>bicycle</u> and <u>tricycle.</u>	I heard on the news about a <u>**vehicle**</u> in a bad accident.

Word Map

Pick a word that was new or hard for you to understand and make a Word Map.

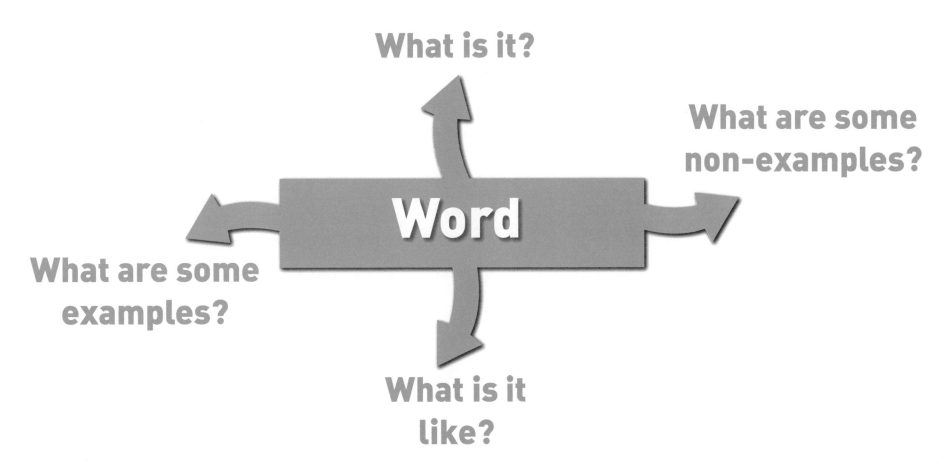

What is it?

What are some non-examples?

Word

What are some examples?

What is it like?

References

Baumann, James, and Edward J. Kame'enui. ***Vocabulary Instruction: Research to Practice***. New York: Guilford Press, 2004.

Bear, Donald, Shane Templeton, Marcia Invernizzi, and Francine Johnson. ***Words Their Way***. New Jersey: Merrill/Prentice Hall, 1998.

Beck, Isabel, Margaret G. McKeown, and Linda Kucan. ***Bringing Words to Life: Robust Vocabulary Instruction***. New York: Guilford Press, 2002.

Blachowicz, Camille. and Peter J. Fisher. ***Teaching Vocabulary in All Classrooms***. New Jersey: Merrill/Prentice Hall, 2002.

Cunningham, Patricia. ***Phonics They Use***. New York: Addison Wesley Longman, 2000.

Nagy, William. ***Teaching Vocabulary to Improve Reading Comprehension***. Newark, NJ: International Reading Association, 1988.

Pinnell, Gay Su and Irene C. Fountas. ***Word Matters***. New Hampshire: Heinemann, 1998.

Promoting Vocabulary Development: Components of Effective Vocabulary Instruction. Austin, TX: Texas Education Agency, 2000.

About the Author

Emily Cayuso is a Campus Instructional Coordinator/Reading Specialist in San Antonio, Texas. She has taught a variety of primary grades and has worked as a Reading Recovery and Title 1 Reading Teacher Specialist over the past thirty-one years. Emily has also served as a part-time adjunct faculty member at the University of Texas in San Antonio working with pre-service teachers. She conducts workshops for reading and language arts teachers. Recognized twice in "Who's Who Among America's Teachers," Emily is the author of ***Designing Teaching Study Groups: A Guide for Success, Flip for Comprehension*** and its Spanish translation, ***Dar La Vuelta a la Comprensión***. She holds a B.S. and an M.Ed.